The Missions: California's Heritage

MISSION SAN ANTONIO
de PADUA

by

Mary Null Boulé

Merryant Publishing
Vashon, Washington

Book Three in a series of twenty-one

JUL   1992

With special thanks to Msgr. Francis J. Weber, Archivist of the Los Angeles Catholic Diocese for his encouragement and expertise in developing this series.

ISBN: 1-877599-02-6

Father Junípero Serra

INTRODUCTION

FATHER SERRA AND THE MISSIONS: AN INTRODUCTION

The year was 1769. On the east coast of what would soon become the United States, the thirteen original colonies were making ready to break away from England. On the west coast of our continent, however, there could be found only untamed land inhabited by Native Americans, or Indians. Although European explorers had sailed up and down the coast in their ships, no one but American Indians had explored the length of this land on foot . . . until now.

To this wild, beautiful country came a group of adventurous men from New Spain, as Mexico was then called. They were following the orders of their king, King Charles III of Spain.

One of the men was a Spanish missionary named Fray Junípero Serra. He had been given a tremendous job; especially since he was fifty-six years old, an old man in those days. King Charles III had ordered mission settlements to be built along the coast of Alta (Upper) California and it was Fr. Serra's task to carry out the king's wishes.

Father Serra had been born in the tiny village of Petra on the island of Mallorca, Spain. He had done such an excellent job of teaching and working with the Indians in Mexican missions, the governor of New Spain had suggested to the king that Fr. Serra do the same with the Indians of Alta California. Hard-working Fray Serra was helped by Don Gaspár de Portolá, newly chosen governor of Alta California, and two other Franciscan priests who had grown up with Fr. Serra in Mallorca, Father Fermin Lasuén and Father Francisco Palóu.

There were several reasons why men had been told to build settlements along the coast of this unexplored country. First, missions would help keep the land as Spanish territory. Spain wanted to be sure the rest of the world knew it owned this rich land. Second, missions were to be built near harbors so towns would grow there. Ships from other countries could then stop to trade with the Spaniards, but these travelers could not try to claim the land for themselves. Third, missions were a good way to turn Indians into Christian, hard-working people.

It would be nice if we could write here that everything went well; that twenty-one missions immediately sprang up along the coast. Unfortunately, all did not go well. It would take fifty-four years to build all the California Missions. During those fifty-four years many people died from Indian attacks, sickness, and starvation. Earthquakes and fires constantly ruined mission buildings, which then had to be built all over again. Fr. Serra calmly overcame each problem as it happened, as did those priests who followed him.

When a weary Fray Serra finally died in 1784, he had founded nine missions from San Diego to Monterey and had arranged the building of many more. Fr. Lasuén continued Fr. Serra's work, adding eight more missions to the California mission chain. The remaining four missions were founded in later years.

Originally, plans had been to place missions a hard day's walk from each other. Many of them were really quite far apart. Travelers truly struggled to go from one mission to another along the 650 miles of walking road known as El Camino Real, The Royal Highway. Today keen eyes will sometimes see tall, curved poles with bells hanging from them sitting by the side of streets and highways. These bell poles are marking a part of the old El Camino Real.

At first Spanish soldiers were put in charge of the towns which grew up near each mission. The priests were told to handle only the mission and its properties. It did not take long to realize the soldiers were not kind and gentle leaders. Many were uneducated and did not have the understanding they should have had in dealing with people. So the padres came to be in charge of not only the mission, but of the townspeople and even of the soldiers.

The first missions at San Diego and Monterey were built near the ocean where ships could bring them needed supplies. After early missions began to grow their own food and care for themselves, later mission compounds were built farther away from the coast. What one mission did well, such as leatherworking, candlemaking, or raising cattle, was shared with other missions. As a result, missions became somewhat specialized in certain products.

Although mission buildings looked different from mission to mission, most were built from one basic plan. Usually a compound was constructed as a large, four-sided building with an inner patio in the center. The outside of the quadrangle had only one or two doors, which were locked at night to protect the mission. A church usually sat at one corner of the quadrangle and was always the tallest and largest part of the mission compound.

Facing the inner patio were rooms for the two priests living there, workshops, a kitchen, storage rooms for grain and food, and the mission office. Rooms along the back of the quadrangle often served as home to the unmarried Indian women who worked in the kitchen. The rest of the Indians lived just outside the walls of the mission in their own village.

Beyond the mission wall and next to the church was a cemetery. Today you can still see many of the original headstones of those who died while living and working at the mission. Also outside the walls were larger workshops, a reservoir holding water used at the mission, and orchards containing fruit trees. Huge fields surrounded each mission where crops grew and livestock such as sheep, cattle, and horses grazed.

It took a great deal of time for some Indian tribes to understand the new way of life a mission offered, even though the

Native Americans always had food and shelter when they became mission Indians. Each morning all Indians were awakened at sunrise by a church bell calling them to church. Breakfast followed church . . . and then work. The women spun thread and made clothes, as well as cooked meals. Men and older boys worked in workshops or fields and constructed buildings. Meanwhile the Indian children went to school, where the padres taught them. After a noon meal there was a two hour rest before work began again. After dinner the Indians sang, played, or danced. This way of life was an enormous change from the less organized Indian life before the missionaries arrived. Many tribes accepted the change, some had more trouble getting used to a regular schedule, some tribes never became a part of mission life.

Water was all-important to the missions. It was needed to irrigate crops and to provide for the mission people and animals. Priests designed and engineered magnificent irrigation systems at most of the missions. All building of aqueducts and reservoirs of these systems was done by the mission Indians.

With all the organized hard work, the missions did very well. They grew and became strong. Excellent vineyards gave wine for the priests to use and to sell. Mission fields produced large grain crops of wheat and corn, and vast grazing land developed huge herds of cattle and sheep. Mission life was successful for over fifty years.

When Mexico broke away from Spain, it found it did not have enough money to support the California missions, as Spain had been doing. So in 1834, Mexico enforced the secularization law which their government had decreed several years earlier. This law stated missions were to be taken away from the missionaries and given to the Indians. The law said that if an Indian did not want the land or buildings, the property was to be sold to anyone who wished to buy it.

It is true the missions had become quite large and powerful. And as shocked as the padres were to learn of the secularization law, they also knew the missions had originally been planned as temporary, or short term projects. The priests had been sure their Indians would be well-trained enough to run the missions by themselves when the time came to move to other unsettled lands. In fact, however, even after fifty years the California Indians were still not ready to handle the huge missions.

Since the Indians did not wish to continue the missions, the buildings and land were sold, the Indians not even waiting for money or, in some cases, receiving money for the sale.

Sad times lay ahead. Many Indians went back to the old way of life. Some Indians stayed on as servants to the new owners and often these owners were not good to them. Mission buildings were used for everything from stores and saloons to animal barns. In one mission the church became a barracks for the army. A balcony was built for soldiers with their horses stabled in the altar area. Rats ate the stored grain and beautiful church robes. Furniture and objects left by the padres were stolen. People even stole the mission building roof tiles, which then caused the adobe brick walls to melt from rain. Earthquakes finished off many buildings.

Shortly after California became a part of the United States in the mid-1860s, our government returned all mission buildings to the Catholic Church. By this time most of them were in terrible condition. Since the priests needed only the church itself and a few rooms to live in, the other rooms of the mission were rented to anyone who needed them. Strange uses were found in some cases. In the San Fernando Mission, for example, there was once a pig farm in the patio area.

Tourists finally began to notice the mission ruins in the early 1900s. Groups of interested people got together to see if the missions could be restored. Some missions had been "modernized" by this time, unfortunately, but within the last thirty years historians have found enough pictures, drawings, and written descriptions to rebuild or restore most of the missions to their original appearances.

The restoration of all twenty-one missions is a splendid way to preserve our California heritage. It is the hope of many Californians that this dream of restoration can become a reality in the near future.

MISSION SAN ANTONIO de PADUA

I. THE MISSION TODAY

San Antonio de Padua is found near the tiny town of Jolón, in the Valley of the Oaks. It is all alone as it was long ago when the missionary priests were in charge. Strange as it might seem, the mission today finds itself right in the middle of a United States military reservation, but no one would ever know. No modern buildings are near it; just the mission quadrangle, many uncovered foundations of buildings which once stood outside the quadrangle, and parts of the irrigation system are found at the mission site. There are even a few trees still there from mission days. Each foundation has been well-marked with signs explaining the use of the buildings of this once huge and successful mission.

As you drive up to the mission you see a well-restored quadrangle, patio, and church. All of the buildings but the convento, which houses the museum, are being used today. How nice to see a "working" mission in this day and age! Francescan priests use the mission as a training center for young men studying to become priests.

Across the front of Mission San Antonio are the customary arches of the corridor. The pillars of the arches are made of kiln-fired tiles, or bricks. Twelve of these arches are the only remainders of the original convento of 1816. Inside the convento is a very fine museum containing objects dug up when the mission was restored in the early 1950 s. Millstones, mortar and pestles, sheep shears; carpenter tools, broken pottery used by the early missionaries, kettles, and objects returned to the mission at the time of rebuilding can all be found in this excellent museum. Most interesting are working models of pieces of machinery used during mission days.

The restored church is built of adobe bricks made from the dust of the original bricks the Indians made in 1810, when this church was first built. The outside walls of the church are six feet thick near the foundation and thin to five feet in thickness near the roof. The building is 200 feet long and 40 feet wide.

Attached to the front of the church is the original facade. This beautiful facade is made of burnt bricks and is the only one of its kind in the mission chain. Three bells hang in the three archways at the top of the facade. The large bell in the center is the only original bell left. Between the facade and the church is a closed-in entrance with a most unusual domed ceiling, also of burned brick.

The inside walls of the church are painted with simple Indian-style fresco decorations like those usually found on church walls during mission days. These walls, along with the front facade, are the only remainders of the original church. On the arch framing the sanctuary are stars painted on a blue background. Above the altar in the sanctuary, the ceiling is painted a lovely bright blue.

The statues of the reredos behind the altar are from the original church. They were kept at Mission San Miguel during the years when no one was living at Mission San Antonio. The paintings hanging on the walls, however, are not those of the early mission days. All of the original paintings have been lost. Those hanging in the church today are paintings from Mission Santa Bárbara and from a collection preserved in Mexico.

The church has a vaulted ceiling which matches the shape of the outside roof. It is made of timbers laid length-wise. This is not the usual type of ceiling for mission churches, however. Most of the other churches have a flat ceiling with the timbers laid cross-wise.

So many people have cared about Mission San Antonio through the years, even when the mission was empty. Because all these people did care so much, the mission today is almost an exact restoration of what it used to be.

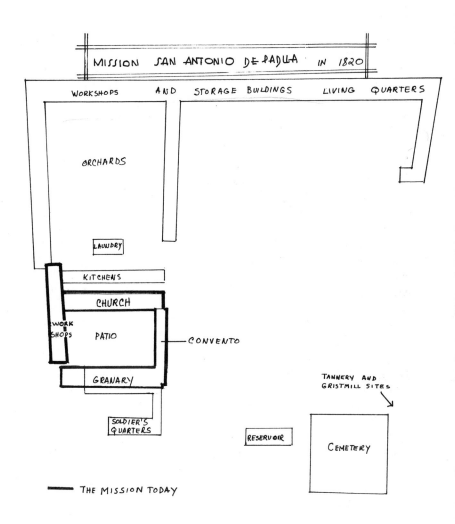

MISSION SAN ANTONIO DE PADUA IN 1820

WORKSHOPS AND STORAGE BUILDINGS LIVING QUARTERS

ORCHARDS

LAUNDRY

KITCHENS

CHURCH

WORK SHOPS

PATIO

CONVENTO

GRANARY

SOLDIER'S QUARTERS

TANNERY AND GRISTMILL SITES

RESERVOIR

CEMETERY

THE MISSION TODAY

II. THE HISTORY OF THE MISSION

The original name given to the mission by Father Junípero Serra was Mission San Antonio de Padua de los Robles. This means Mission St. Anthony of Padua of the Oaks. There was a good reason for Fr. Serra to pick such a long name for this, his third mission. The valley chosen for the building of Mission San Antonio had huge, beautiful oak trees. It was a lovely setting for a mission.

On July 14, 1771, bells were hung from one of the large oak trees. A small altar had just been set up when suddenly Fr. Serra, who was in charge, was overcome with joy. He began ringing the bells loudly and called to Indians to join him. The few priests and military men around him were quite surprised since the valley seemed empty of any humans but them.

But there actually was one young Indian watching and he became so curious that he came out of hiding. Father Serra gave gifts to the Indian and treated him so kindly that the young boy brought members of his tribe to meet Fr. Serra. Even though the Indians could not understand Fr. Serra's words, they did like his gentleness. These friendly Indians were always helpful and loyal through all the years Mission San Antonio was a working mission.

Father Serra left two very fine priests, Fr. Miguel Pieras and Fr. Buenaventura Sitjar, at the site to begin building the mission. Both priests remained at the mission until their deaths, but Fr. Sitjar actually stayed at Mission San Antonio for 37 years! He is the main reason this was one of the largest and most successful of all the missions. He was an excellent leader and the Indians loved him. Fr. Sitjar took time to learn the Mutsun language spoken by the Indians of that area. Over the years he wrote down the Indian words and the strange throat-clearing sounds needed to pronounce each word in a dictionary. After he died his dictionary was found at the mission and was published.

At first the two priests had to do most of the work of beginning the mission buildings themselves, but the Indians helped as they could. Then, in 1773, the mission was moved to where it is today. More water was found at the present site, and water to irrigate their crops was badly needed. This time more people came to help with the building.

By 1774, records show that 178 Indians lived at the mission. There were also 68 cattle and seven horses. The Indians and soldiers were living in wood and tule houses and a small church had been built. There were workshops of adobe brick, also. The church we see today, however, was not built until 1810 - 1813. It was the third church built by the early missionaries.

Water was what was needed the most in the dry Valley of the Oaks. The San Antonio River was the only river in the valley and it became almost dry each summer. Because of the hot, dry summers, the padres, or priests, thought up an amazing irrigation system to keep their crops watered until harvest time. Fr. Sitjar had a dam built across the river at a place high in the mountains. Water was brought down from the dam in brick lined tunnels to reservoirs near the mission. Wells were dug. A water-powered mill was even built in 1806, using the irrigation system to grind the grain for the mission. This is said to be the first mill in California having a horizontal power wheel.

Because of the great need for water, the mission had huge rancheros many miles away from it. Large herds of cattle, horses, and sheep grazed on the pastures of these rancheros. The animals the mission raised here were of a very good quality and San Antonio actually became quite famous for the excellent horses bred there.

During its most successful time, between 1802 and 1805, the mission had 1,300 Indians living and working there. Some of the shops to be found at the mission at that time were a weavery, a room for carding and spinning wool, a tannery for treating leather, a carpenter shop, a stable, and a harness shop.

1825 was the year of great rains. It rained so hard that many of the buildings collapsed. The priests in charge, Fr. Sancho and Fr. Cabot, rebuilt the buildings, making them stronger than before. Records show that in 1827 there were 7,362 head of cattle; 11,000 sheep; 500 mares and colts; and 300 tamed horses. In 1829 a visitor described the mission as being in "perfect order". He said the Indians were well-dressed and

15

the workshops busy and tidy. Mission life went on this way until 1834, when the missions were taken from the priests by the Mexican government. This was called secularization. Unfortunately, the mission Indians were not ready to care for the mission by themselves, so by 1841 there were only 150 Indians left at Mission San Antonio. What is more, only 800 cattle, 2,000 sheep, and 500 horses remained.

Life at the mission became even sadder. The Mexican governor of California offered all the missions for sale to anyone interested in owning one. Many missions were bought, but no one wanted to buy Mission San Antonio. A Mexican priest by the name of Father Dorotea Ambris was sent to care for it when President Lincoln returned the missions to the Catholic Church in 1851. Fr. Ambris did his best to keep the mission from falling apart during the thirty-one years he stayed there. He finally died in 1882, and the mission was left alone. People stole everything they could from the buildings. Even roof tiles, timbers, and locks off the doors were taken. The mission remained empty, except for owls and bats, until only the church facade and walls and some of the arches of the convento were left standing.

In 1903 an effort was made to rebuild the church, but earthquakes and no money caused work being done on it to stop. It took almost fifty years after that time before it was truly restored. Francescan priests returned to the mission in 1929, but they could not find enough money to do more than repair little things. The Hearst Foundation finally came to the rescue in the 1940s with a gift of $50,000 to repair the church. Then more people gave money to help restore the quadrangle as well.

At the time of restoration many mission objects were found and brought back. Among the things found was one of the original bells. It is the large center bell in the facade, named Osquila. The roof tiles were also found, but these could not be returned because they are set in cement. They can be seen to this day on the roof of the Burlingame railroad station.

Even without the original roof tiles, the Mission San Antonio de Padua is one of the most faithfully restored of the missions. Best of all, it is not surrounded by a busy city. It still sits alone in its beautiful Valley de los Robles just as it did during mission days.

Sanctuary of restored church. Notice ceiling shaped to the slope of the roof, and ceiling boards running lengthwise.

The only remaining tree from mission days is this pomegranate tree. It still bears fruit.

OUTLINE OF SAN ANTONIO

I. The mission today
A. Location of mission
B. Description of location
C. Restoration complete
   1. Foundations uncovered and labeled
D. Mission is a "working" mission
   1. Francescan training center
E. Excellent museum
   1. Artifacts and working machine models
F. Outside of church
   1. Adobe brick from dust of original brick used
   2. Walls' thickness
   3. Original facade of burnt brick
      a. Three archways in facade hold three bells
   4. Size of church
G. Church, inside
   1. Wall designs
   2. Ceiling built differently (length-wise timbers)
      a. Painted bright color
   3. Archway decoration
   4. Reredos statues
   5. Paintings on walls

II. History of mission

A. Original long name and why
B. Founding
   1. Founding date
   2. Young Indian
C. Type of Indians living there
D. Father Sitjar
   1. Kind of leader he was
   2. His dictionary
E. Change of mission site in 1773
   1. Why the change
F. The mission in 1774
   1. Buildings found there
G. Present-day church begun 1810

Outline continued next page

H. Irrigation system built
  1. Description of system
  2. Water-powered mill
  3. Rancheros for animals
  4. Mission's fine horses
I. Mission's most successful years
  1. Number of Indians at that time
  2. Kinds of workshops
J. Problems of 1825
  1. Frs. Cabot and Sancho
K. Mission in 1829
L. Secularization in 1834
  1. Indians leave, too; why?
M. Mission returned to Catholic Church
  1. Fr. Ambris arrives
  2. How long Fr. Ambris stays
N. Mission empty for over forty years
  1. People steal from it
  2. Only facade, walls, and some archways left
O. Restoration first tried in 1903
P. Priests return in 1929
  1. Have no money to restore mission
Q. Hearst Foundation gives $50,000 in 1940s
R. Restoration finished
  1. Many objects given back for restoration

GLOSSARY

BUTTRESS: a large mass of stone or wood used to strengthen buildings

CAMPANARIO: a wall which holds bells

CLOISTER: an enclosed area; a word often used instead of convento

CONVENTO: mission building where priests lived

CORRIDOR: covered, outside hallway found at most missions

EL CAMINO REAL: highway between missions; also known as The King's Highway

FACADE: front wall of a building

FONT: large, often decorated bowl containing Holy Water for baptizing people

FOUNDATION: base of a building, part of which is below the ground

FRESCO: designs painted directly on walls or ceilings

LEGEND: a story coming from the past

PORTICO: porch or covered outside hallway

PRESERVE: to keep in good condition without change

PRESIDIO: a settlement of military men

QUADRANGLE: four-sided shape; the shape of most missions

RANCHOS: large ranches often many miles from mission proper where crops were grown and animal herds grazed

REBUILD: to build again; to repair a great deal of something

REPLICA: a close copy of the original

REREDOS: the wall behind the main altar inside the church

*RESTORATION: to bring something back to its original condition (see * below)

SANCTUARY: area inside, at the front of the church where the main altar is found

SECULARIZATION: something not religious; a law in mission days taking the mission buildings away from the church and placing them under government rule

*ORIGINAL: the first one; the first one built

BIBLIOGRAPHY

Bauer, Helen. *California Mission Days.* Sacramento, CA: California State Department of Education, 1957.

Goodman, Marian. *Missions of California.* Redwood City, CA: Redwood City Tribune, 1962.

Rohder, Padre Regis, O.F.M. *Mission San Antonio.* Jolon, CA: Francescan Padres, no date.

Sunset Editors. *The California Missions.* Menlo Park, CA: Lane Publishing Company, 1979.

Weber, Msgr. Francis J. *Mission in the Sierras.* Hong Kong: Libra Press Limited, no date.

Wright, Ralph B., ed. *California Missions.* Arroyo Grande, CA 93420: Hubert A. Lowman, 1977.

For more information about this mission, write to:

Mission San Antonio de Padua
Jolon, CA 93928

It is best to enclose a self-addressed, stamped envelope and a small amount of money to pay for brochures and pictures the mission might send you.

CREDITS

Cover art and Father Serra Illustration: Ellen Grim
Illustrations: Alfredo de Batuc
Ground Layout: Mary Boulé